"He saw. / She saw." Anne Waldman and Vincent Katz say. If seeing is an act of love, Waldman and Katz not only love but "love to be astonished". And they collapse the many eras of New York into a mural of music and reminiscence… embrace it!

—Francesco Clemente

*Fantastic Caryatids* is a wonderful conversation between two poets. The combined poetry is magical and the conversation in the second part of the book opens up doors of recognition and reminiscence. A total pleasure.

—Pat Steir

# Fantastic Caryatids

# Fantastic Caryatids

**Anne Waldman & Vincent Katz**

A Conversation with Art

BlazeVOX [books] / Buffalo, NY

Fantastic Caryatids: A Conversation with Art
by Anne Waldman and Vincent Katz
Copyright © 2017

Published by BlazeVOX [books]

Cover Photograph by Vincent Katz

All rights reserved. No part of this book may be reproduced without
the publisher's written permission, except for brief quotations in reviews.

Printed in the United States of America

Design and typesetting by Heloisa Zero
Photographs by Vincent Katz
The fonts used are Futura and Gill Sans
Thanks to Oliver Katz for assistance

First Edition
ISBN: 978-1-60964-244-0
Library of Congress Control Number: 2015959393

BlazeVOX [books]
131 Euclid Ave
Kenmore, NY 14217

Editor@blazevox.org

*publisher of weird little books*
# BlazeVOX [ books ]
blazevox.org

21 20 19 18 17 16 15 14 13 12 01 02 03 04 05 06 07 08 09 10

For Ambrose, Oliver, and Isaac

and

In Memory of Edwin Denby,

who also loved these streets —

*Colored autumn long ago vanished unheard*
*Raspberry afterglows viewed from Twenty-third*
*Bluish mist midtown as in ruins of Rome*
*Forest mornings in Manhattan, my home*

# Contents

Fantastic Caryatids                                9

Anne Waldman & Vincent Katz:
A Conversation                                     31

# Fantastic Caryatids

Look at that field
I love that field, late in flower
And trees that head the precinct
Queen Anne's Lace bedeck in rhythms unforetold
I feel the wind embracing me
And am ready for the season

Thought of the act of seeing with one's own eyes
Thought of Brakhage trance, how it is an affect of desire
Filmic, fleeting, fragile, focused and it goes on without its manliness:
Of sifting days for a clue, don't go modern on me
Of deprivation in urban corners, and the lushness too,
Of the past, of us, our time, of our composite generation
And its dimension as a weed might have
None, you could say, or…
A map of Calvino's cities, how that is magical and a ride
Thought as we sat in the café of both the inadequacy
And the necessity of poetry, of the gallery space
We might visit that can hold one mind and name the local

That is a shift, seasonal, continental,
Brings generation's urge to conflate
Desire and camaraderie, was that
The '70s, Loulou de la Falaise, or
The teens, a name not yet known,
A name becoming

This is Idriss, this is Monotony, a small village
This is a capital town: Morovodor you could invent where
    *mouchoirs* are both common and rare

This is Inventory and this is the city of Gnosis, barren
With its bite gone
This is the small burg of Reticent
Housing a little museum with stalks of filaments
Like flags
Then metal creeps in: This is another town: Gorbuduc named
    for a poem by John Ashbery
When I look inside I see a topiary garden, short on humans
And the results come streaming in

Is it my destination the way you say "truly"?
Do people get in the way of looking at art?
Is Emilie Clark painting a new animal that grows a deeper nature?
Is art ready for vision even?

What is the question of questions about mind—
That it recedes? That you care?
That it's all in the light
If you could behave
If you could let go
What have you seen before that tempts you
Color, closeness, habit is it?

Or hunger in the blind eye?

I call to Vincent an Edwin memory
What he captures of it
And what is its time to come

He saw.
She saw.

*BRUNCH. DINNER. FUERZA BRUTA.*

Mini Corinthian columns support arches support flying butterfly brickwork

Long live our mattress!

Can you believe Times Square?

Everything so cleaned-up now façade at least

Times Square is angles, planes interact, shuttle into space

(…The occasional derelict building)

Above our eyes, fantastic caryatids, artists always get in under the gun

They force the necessary — big bucks give way to beauty

Design gives them clout

Macy's proportions of window lights metal frame decorative

Look up! See towers that are this city's homes

No picket fence here, look up!

And look to detail in the building: arch, balcony, indent

But down below, or out a window, that other, always-demanding-of-attention:

People, humans going about their business

The way they look now

Look: long, short, hair crowd outside PIZZA, the Continental

Custom-made clothing: blue, red, yellow hats

Night now glow from lights, faded more odd fragments built into brick

*I WANNA ROCK WITH YOU*

Seeing again, how people look, now
Time has changed again, it's no longer ten years ago, or five

Over the bridge, jagged lights, spatters,
Even skyline blurred, but heavy
And there go the lights

Always feeling that life's going on down there
Got to go after it

See what it says

What you see through rain, Anne, and rain, rain again —

I haven't forgotten your call:

A memory

Edwin

On 23$^{rd}$ in the night

We met by chance as I was coming home (but why to 23$^{rd}$?)

And he pointed out a restaurant he used to go to

Then walked off, and I too, walked into the past

Back to those stores, those restaurants, smells


    distant spots
    through dark and orange
    autumns past
    day painting color on park
    yellows, greens, highlit

    light patch on lawn:
    bright green on dark

    trees, yellow-green, are hit
    reddish vines climb cyclone fence

mothers walk kids to school
some scooter, some bike
people walk dogs to music

hidden tenor sax from some southern corner

further and further highlights, as day arises
further sights of walkers

squarish rust library fronts park
also receives day's slanting highlights

then suddenly the hurricane is coming to town
and it's early
in the long wait:
stock up, get more batteries, plug in the cell
get all the "juice" you can, stored up for hours,
be safe, batten down the hatches
the way the day turns a miracle remembering all intense weathers
and you stare into the grey city your beast, a burden to monitor
where I was, where we were, what was going on
in the heart of any poetry reading social moment
who one was in love with in the wind, in the proverbial storm

Acropolis maidens glow anew
on 23rd or Spring or 75th
hitting the ceiling, then moving up

κόροι καὶ κόραι
six sisters stood
one kidnapped, other five heard in lamentation
from afar, the near: nothing
silent rock, Ionic columns,
ironic women

with Edwin in the heavy rain after the ballet,
the night Suzanne Farrell took a spill
but she was so extraordinary so poised now you see it now you don't
and did it really happen is that what we saw
a brief crumple in the pleat of sublime ballet time
oh! and is she hurt, who comes to pick her up but her own resilience
what we saw or did we? and forgave, her error, her mishap —
was it? really? Suzanne?
what was it? faulty shoe, flawed floor, or a mote of dust,
hair filament fell from ballerina's faultless bun,
her off-guard, split-time, what was she thinking? was
she counting? did she skip a beat?

I forget the score but it doesn't matter
Edwin gave a little gasp
it became exalted moment of radical beauty she could
fail and fall like the rest of us
from a perfect heaven
Balanchine's reigning queen, we watched her every move
slightest neck muscle tremble,
long strain of leg out   out   out
a leap, closure and she *was* us in some way, our gaze intense on her
and I loved her mousey face and funny voice when she spoke in a TV
interview
and then didn't want to hear, see, more, her power her force diminished by
mundane tone dare I say that?   who is the real woman —
a fabricant?

and the glorious weather days off from school
like precious golden time outside time
like now and what do I see outside time
doldrums

Panic at election time
The best man has got to win, you see?
Don't you see, US of America?
The Empire State is turned off right now, what color tonight?
I want all the galleries & museums to open up
This could be the end of the world, so let's go on a seeing spree

*Le bodhisattva Avalokiteśvara aux mille bras, Cinq Dynasties.*

*"Brian Boru" Harp: This 14th or 15th century harp is*
*the oldest surviving Irish harp and has been erroneously*
*associated with Brian Boru, king of Ireland (died 1014).*
*It is made of willow and has 29 strings.*

*Che juega una partida de ajedrez en la Ciudad Deportiva*
*(Palais de Sports), 1961.*

*Cattedrale di S. Maria Assunta*
*Isola di Torcello*
*Universal Judgement – Mosaic of the XII-XIII century.*
*Detail.*

Can chlorine kill someone?

flotation rotation
flotation device
devise a system
rote beyond system
hex hegemony
a worldly system

Light coming over haze
Endless body walking
Weather cool but calm
Strange look in the eye
Poetry keep it on level
Calm being on street
Our city, country even
Now, populace spoken
*On level?*

Right taken from right

True being is the heart

Don't clutch but desire

Fifth Avenue, my youth
Should one go west or north?

Happy that one moment
With two friends near park
Smell of leaves anticipated
Aura of adrenaline

Form is more than shape
More than static position of components
In a whole

Form is love

*Listening to you I get the music*
*Gazing at you I feel the heat*
*Following you I climb the mountain*
*I get excitement at your feet*

*Right behind you I see the millions*
*On you I see the glory*
*From you I get opinions*
*From you I get the story*

story is seeing — Happy Monday —
sensing the way this edge of park
creates sensitivities within or against
pushes environmental-political, age

here is enclave, there devastation
sound of working, machine, buses, trucks
nexus-circle of jazz, design, residence, war
presided over by CNN Golden Victory chariot

houses of worship, ultimately
style — in clothing, poetry, war —
inside coming out

how trenchant insouciance could be
in that look, gaze of the "subject" as it clears space
directly at you and these subjects-poets (could be) or brilliant glamorous women
   a studied detail of dress, hair, mouth a red you can't resist

& industrious

*pugnativity* — a word I'll make up and command —
   of Frank O'Hara's nose
cutting into space

& I thought of William Carlos Williams's flowers

and void of complexity that is tricky because
it's very complex — a composition that radiates the will to
   greet I mean "salute" (Jimmy Schuyler)  the day

how are we to survive our crave for image & "ruse"?

enjoy
walk
pace
leap, primate
stop and start
and love
to be startled
through
amusement
of a new angle
here
with
wife Katie
of
painter Schneeman
who
should
be
included
in
this
display
of
portraiture

stand before "Ted"
   is this the way

I immortalize him?

Possibly, did Alex?

stand before a flat surface that suddenly
resists
easy
dimension
declension
appreciate the *poiesis*

familiar hand at face
a "thinking" gesture
& related to
being one with a beard
or self-aggrandizing element

& author of
beautiful lines that
separate themselves out

singular
entities
literally "cut-out" of life
as sonnets pasted out of past
warm encumbrance of line
of tempest of quivering Rimbaud

clusters that are not bombs

but bursts of heart
or books
reference to the greatness of others
newly devised

the "arrangement" we say

of a mind in
"love with poetry"

O! and the artifacts therein

(As Karyatis she rejoiced in the
Dance of the nut-tree villages of Karyai,
Carrying on head
A basket of live reeds
As if they were dancing plants…)

Did Alkamenes scale desire's height
to see said women erect, challenge
to anyone, or was it squarely conceived
to prop Erechtheion, edifice sacred to

Athena, Poseidon, and the first kings?

theory & practice, my DNA

this will get you far

& it did, it does, says Berrigan

*the whole ride*

"seeing" is why we exist for a time

and would you agree, holding up
the world in imagination

the shapes and colors need greater
scrutiny

how many years later
do things, time, do it?

In 1979, read an article they'd
been removed to safety in *mouseion*
amusing to think on muse
as was Loulou to Yves
or so many other


Individual thrusts or bursts of identity

Become masterpieces

Ask our bodies

Doing the work

How does time pass in this
  segment

Like a movie

Like an instinct you can't stop

Control will get you nowhere

A rubric of comedy needed here

I will laugh again, I swear

& tickle a younger generational bone

No need to turn back the clock

Sites of satisfaction everywhere in a
    lost world where the comic is serious

Perhaps the most is *le mot juste*

Did they cry out *We just want to be understood?*

Never

*

"I can see the little fists / and the rocking-horse motion of her breasts."

*

we walked and saw persistence of vision

I saw you inside before you saw me seeing

I tried to catch your attention

but you were busy being an active New Yorker

taking care of her space, business, poetry

in the gallery, surrounded by faces

and in between the faces seeing:

white breasts and curves of color

then collage of poet and art

another poet other Emily

soon spoons of Poons

wrapped us in their spools

but we refused their names

name so much a part of art

separate tedious fork in road

Yvonne's about looking

so hard looking gets

looped, gets crunched, gets looked at

reduced and mutable

but substance! substance! the livelong day

pushed into some other space

where one can fly again, unbound

by preconception, or so it seemed

racing the freeway by river

our city again, ode, paean, to

which is flexible is epigrammatic is

self is non-self is cellular is phenotype

is radial is symmetry is not is not

is invader is relationship is epistemological

build the software of city?

is luster is expensive is psychodynamic

is its watertowers its variants its hypertext

not Cyclops but old new thing in time

an undead tale of teenage fear

came dirt to mask

again confronted ones

by structures

and art inside buildings

and poetry which floats free

if you retain in memory

and ownership of discourse

a palace that breathes

what is that word that reeks of advertising?

has no business in what we are trying

women — minus one —

gleam, glow, in clothing

of course not ownership but they

blight, blunt, less aggressive

senses  Hooray!  Hooray!

for undefinability!

for incoherence!

for archaic television!

for cared-for jumble!

for elegant flotation!

Culture as well as
Implication
In nar
Storie
Redu
An
Genom
Bio
Modest
Minded, single
Dis-
Breakdown
Heart
Rapt
Post Post-mod

Balzac would like this
perspicacity of figures at attention
in conversation or psychological distance
*distress?* hardly
but no more parties
but this we have:
Alex's generous angle and lit
flat gorgeous facial plane a song
a map, a color field
what are the colors of all flesh
flashing by
heads into space once again
no more parties but art?
we could be bumpkins
out-of-towners
cross the tracks
come to drink at
shrine of art
as sex is remaindered
in the video
a cross-wire

and someone else dies
central to this slice of time
who made a few reputations
and heads turned…

*don't walk away, Rene*

*(Rene Ricard hated that song!) (Which song?) (Blondie?) (Eraserhead?)*

your quip
& quixotic metabolism

*Amazone (detail)*
*Römische Marmorkopie*
*Greichisches Original um 430 v Chr.*

Frank O'Hara adored the Roman copies…

Missing caryatid installed in London
Elgin, ambassador to Ottoman
their tits point forward, their hips rock right to left
sawed off the porch and shipped to Scotland
and a mixed message show
with no poets included
& labels waiting to be
archivally written

may I do my rant here?
(complex problem of abstraction)

*if you are going to have*
*these historic anthologies*
*e.g. Holly's Hollywood*
*need to remember the poets*
*who entered at Greene too and*

*did the comparable work
essence of word
ghost of word
poem as overreach ok!*

*Seated Bodhisattva Avalokiteśvara (Guanyin)
11th Century, Chinese, Northern Song dynasty.*

Rene, don't walk away, we miss you

1687: nicked by bullet and debris
during Turk-Venetian contest

 & I'll walk you home tonight, Eileen

mixed threads, *mixotricha*, of evening
street raw with inter-discipline

have seen it all: an enormous fire
set in 1st c. BC by Sulla
nearby dynamite explosion gods chose not to hear
they looked toward the Aegean
women condemned in penance
hometown Caryae sided with Persia

art in a new light

smooth or wrinkled

tall or short

traits

or were they young dancers?
as Anne Teresa de Keersmaeker's in "Elena's Aria"?

under Ottoman, a harem

pragmatically

rise

most

linguistically

code

life

locates

see?

ties

eyes

what did we miss?

# Anne Waldman & Vincent Katz

## A Conversation with Art

## Anne Waldman & Vincent Katz : A Conversation with Art

**VK:** Alright, we're live.

**AW:** Live at the Philip Pearlstein show in Chelsea, on 25th Street. We just walked across the street from the extraordinary Jim Dine show of expansive work. These paintings by Philip are quite interesting. As Vincent, my companion on this little jaunt, has noted, the figures seem somewhat drained and as if they're maybe overexposed under fluorescent light, as though they're in some kind of sauna. Interesting compositions: details of various elements of texture and fabric, rugs and kimonos and objects, statues. What else? — a little weather vane, children's toys.

**VK:** That one over there says "readings," as in reading your fortune I guess, and there's a hand with wires attached to it.

**AW:** Ah, and other words in the palm of the hand. Let's see what it says. "Loveline, headline, lifeline," yes. Hmm.

**VK:** It looks like it turns as it goes around, and the fingers go up and down. Maybe you spin it.

**AW:** Yes, maybe they're spun or cranked. Do you think maybe they're cranked?

**VK:** Yes, it looks like it. And she's sitting there in front of it. She's awake. Most of them seem to be asleep, or just without any energy. She's awake, but she seems a little bored, don't you think?

**AW:** Yeah, maybe a little bored. She's probably held that stance for quite a while.

**VK:** And what do you think? It always seems as if the objects are encroaching upon them, that they're inflicting something on them.

**AW:** Yes, they're decorative objects, or maybe folk art to some extent, and yet they're around them, on top of them, behind them, very purposefully, obviously for the compositional effect. Also there's this Southwestern motif. Let's see what else.

**VK:** I like this one a lot, with this inflatable, clear, plastic chair that the foreground model is sitting on. I like the relationship of her body to the viewer: we are looking over her shoulder, as opposed to looking at her, as we are in most of the others.

**AW:** I like the right hand coming onto her breast, onto her chest too. There's more of an intention there, less languid perhaps.

**VK:** There's almost a humorous element too with the second model lying back on a figure, I don't know if it's Native American.

**AW:** Yeah, or Aztec-ian, sort of.

**VK:** But he looks like he's leaning in to support her.

**AW:** Maybe it's another blown-up plastic punch-up doll.

**VK:** I remember the term "pre-Columbian," do you remember that term?

**AK:** Yes, I do remember pre-Columbian. A vast unknown mysterious stretch of time and art.

**VK:** I remember that many years ago Philip's son, I think he was a teenager at the time, but somehow he had become very interested in pre-Columbian art, and he was studying it.

**AW:** Oh, I didn't know that. Maybe then this comes from his son's world, some connection to it.

**VK:** There are some native carpets on the floor there, which is reminding me of the fact that some of these carpets were used for, or included in, some other-worldly, out-of-the-body experiences, such as peyote experiences.

**AW:** Yeah, the designs have directional qualities and may represent the five trajectories of space, I'm not sure. The striated rug that looks simpler, but even that eagle, that's a feather pattern I think, the appliqué piece there. And we have a Mickey Mouse… It's nice when you see the letters, the bits of letters. I enjoy that. That's another inflatable thing, a mattress.

**VK:** I like the very modern elements juxtaposed with the antique.

**AW:** Right, right. Or even folk art. I keep seeing folk art. This boat, I don't know what's behind these horses, but this old toy.

**VK:** There's a toy, a lot of them have propellers, I've noticed. This one has a propeller, and then as you spin the propeller I guess…

**AW:** They move, they cut the log, the axe goes up and down, the signals. Working toys. Funny top-hats.

**VK:** So it's a weird kind of Americana, in which these models are, again, entwined.

**AW:** Entwined, this one even has a tattoo of some kind that almost looks like it's very surfacey, like the model didn't really have a tattoo, it's hard to know.

**VK:** We're coming from the Jim Dine show of "purely abstract" paintings, and then the Thomas Nozkowski exhibition, and we were talking about the different kinds of energy in Dine's show, and I was saying that I saw some sexual imagery pulsing from those former hearts. The Nozkowski show seemed to be decorative in a way, very much involved with shape and form that was very defined.

**AW:** And a similar scale, a smaller scale, like patches of things. This Pearlstein show doesn't seem, despite all these naked bodies, particularly erotic, but the bodies feel more on an equal plateau with the various other elements and objects that are more transient but have these historic and weighted meanings and contexts of decorative art and time and space, rugs and wooden figures and children's toys.

**VK:** But they do feel human, the women. You feel a tenderness towards them in a human way, though not in an erotic way.

**AW:** Right, and they're not young nubile bodies. That's actually what I like about them, they're not glamorized at all. They're a little sleepy, except for this one on the left. Their eyes are closed.

**VK:** What else did we want to talk about, from some of our earlier emails?

**AW:** There's something about your first hit of poetry. I know you grew up with an artist.

**VK:** Well, I have a specific memory I wanted to tell you about. One of those things you remember as a kid because they are mathematical. Joe Brainard came over, probably with Kenward, to the loft on 5th Ave and 23rd, and I remember having this thought go through my head that "Joe is 25, and I'm five." It was just a random fact, but somehow it made an impression on me. There was lots of poetry just lying around the house, and I remember sometimes my Mom would put it underneath the pile of books, because there was some stuff that was pretty triple-X rated, some cartoons and texts. I remember a story actually. It was a column, like "About Town," but it was a downtown version of that, and I remember it vividly. It said something like, "We met at a party, and half an hour later we were in bed together." And it was two people we knew who were not officially together!

**AW:** How much older were you?

**VK:** Not that much older, because it was in the same loft, and we left there when I was about eight. So it was whenever I started reading, seven, eight.

**AW:** You must have been reading early too, I would think.

**VK:** I started reading at six or something. I remember that first hit of reading, I remember that living room area there, a magazine and just being able to read a sentence, and all of a sudden just this incredible charge.

**AW:** So what did you think of that sentence about meeting somebody?

**VK:** I thought it was fun, it just sounded like fun. That was how it was written, the tone of it, it wasn't written like this was some intense, scary, unseemly, or even revolutionary thing. It was just like they were having fun. But, so, to get to my first poetry, it's pretty clear, it was an Ed Sanders poem called "Elm Fuck Poem." That was my first vivid experience with poetry, and it's telling because that connected, and it was both words actually. It was "fuck," but it was also "elm," because I knew elm trees from Maine, and it was a poem about the crotch of the tree, and it's this erotic, Greek, dryadic earth experience. And that was the first poem I read that I could tell was contemporary, because of the way he put those words and those ideas together.

**AW:** Wonderful, that's a very good example. Radical but appropriate for a precocious child who, well, clearly, it's something that wasn't being withheld from you. It was around. That you would open it, and that somehow your eye lit on that seems auspicious.

**VK:** How about you?

**AW:** My parents were readers, my mother more into poetry. Scary Mother Goose. The woman who had her skirt sheared off. We had a library with modernist work and some later folks. W.B. Yeats, A.R. Ammons, Langston Hughes, Wallace Stevens. Poetry was used for official civic occasions at P.S. 8 on King Street. Talk about trees, I remember writing a poem for Arbor Day, and also having to recite "I think that I shall never see / A poem lovely as a tree." Dreadful. And you'd plant a tree. I think we were carrying little trees in buckets. Early eco-poethics. Talk about Greek, you know, dryadic, some little hint of ceremony around poetry. Poetry was trotted out for these occasions. So I had some idea early on that poetry would take place in public space, and also you could write an occasional poem around a subject or a theme. I think those were the kind of assignments; it's not as if we were at that age studying prosody yet.

**VK:** I never had that experience at that age, and certainly that is a major role that poetry has had.

**AW:** Yes, we had Frost at Kennedy's inauguration. Bush Jr. did away with the inaugural poem for his ceremony, and I was more offended by that than some of his other horrific antics. I mean these public things can be really awful as well. But I'm all for poetry at weddings, funerals, births, Thanksgiving, etc. Dinner parties where everyone has to read. But you know every time I've ever planted anything it's accompanied by a poem.

**VK:** Do you remember any early poetry assignments that you had in school?

**AW:** In Junior High, a "Where are the snows of yesteryear?" kind of poem, some haiku, something in French class to do with the "Song of Roland," so a taste of epic. I was quite involved with the student magazines, student publications, and wrote book reviews.

**VK:** What was the first contemporary poetry or modern poetry that you read?

**AW:** Probably Allen's "Howl," Ferlinghetti's "Christ Climbed Down," before the *New American Poetry* anthology. My family subscribed to the *Evergreen Review*. At school, we had the modernists, some e.e. cummings, so that was something that looked a little different, Pound's "The River Merchant's Wife," obligatory Williams, Wallace Stevens, and maybe some things you would expect. No Gertrude Stein as yet. More of the official verse folks came when I went to Bennington, as Howard Nemerov was my teacher, and poets coming through were John Berryman, May Swenson, Richard Wilbur, and we were reading Lowell and so on. I loved "Imitations." But I also got a terrific dose of Blake with Nemerov and classes in Milton, Pope, and Keats and other Romantics.

**VK:** But so was your first real hit the *New American Poetry*?

**AW:** That was the antithesis to what had been presented, and it was most welcome. Because there was a sense of communities in that book, poets in activity together, in the conversation. A company of friends, as Creeley would say. Some of this had been in the air. Beats. Frank O'Hara. I had already looked at *This Kind of Bird Flies Backwards* (Diane di Prima). I met her when I was 17. My father had met Allen in the late '50s I think. There had been some exchange there, Allen possibly visiting Pace University where my

father taught. I remember hearing Lowell at N.Y.U. I remember going up to the YMHA to hear Marianne Moore (my mother was a fan). There was some acknowledgment of the Beat stuff, it was all happening in actual time. My father had read *On the Road*, and maybe some Burroughs, and he had lived in Provincetown next door to John Dos Passos. There was a literary world around my father's bohemian music existence at the time. Before the war, he was a freelance musician; it wasn't until he went off to war and came back from Germany that he went to N.Y.U. on the G.I. Bill and got his doctorate at Columbia and then became a teacher. So a lot of it was what was at home and what was being presented by my parents. I loved *Alice in Wonderland* — if anything, that was the young first hit of outrageous poetry. I would say that *Alice in*

41

*Wonderland* was the most exciting thing out there, wild and strange. What were "slithy toves," or what was a "vorpal sword"? "Mome raths"? I played Alice in a production at The Greenwich House Children's Theatre when I was 10 or 11.

**VK:** I have a memory in school of discovering the poetic trick. Did you ever have that feeling, like, I have this trick that I've learned now that I can use?

**AW:** Well, you have to sum up at the end with some kind of home run. Or sometimes repeat the first line as the last line, or maybe a metaphor that could somehow get extended? I was never very good at that.

**VK:** Yeah, all those things.

**AW:** What was your trick?

**VK:** Well, I think I was in the third grade. I went to Downtown Community School, which was right across the street from St. Mark's Church, and the teacher said, I want you all to write a poem, look around, and I don't remember how she phrased it but I knew that what she wanted us to do was use either metaphor or simile, she was wanting us to invent language. So I looked out the window at St. Mark's Church, and I saw the cast iron fence there with all those points sticking up, and I wrote something like, "The fence posts lined up like so many soldiers at attention." And she said, "This is great!" That's what she was looking for.

**AW:** Why did you think it was a trick?

**VK:** Well, I meant trick in a good sense, because when use techniques, now we call them techniques, but they're things that we know are going to have a certain effect. And now hopefully we use them

42

unconsciously going for something, but I think when you're that young, or you're just starting out, it's interesting to have a conscious awareness of, oh I did this or I can do this, language can do it, it can have a desired effect. It's just that I knew what the person wanted, and I did it.

**AW:** Did you feel some pleasure in having this acknowledged?

**VK:** I did, yeah. I would think that I'd feel cheap, like it was a cheap trick. But I don't really. It was an interesting discovery.

**AW:** I'll never be able to look at those gates at St. Mark's Church in the same way now, Vincent, this is most exciting. I wish I had seen them that way. I remember, of course, in the early days of The Poetry Project, the whole infrastructure business of having to take care and lock the gates and double check. In those days as you may remember, there were grave robberies, and theft of some of our equipment, typewriters and the like, and the hiring of the Pinkerton men. We had to lock up the offices in a particular way. Security was always an issue. The gate was locked and it was sometimes hard to bolt the — not a bolt but, a wooden bar in the cold, the block would be hard, it would be stiff and hard to open and close.

**VK:** Somehow, it was arranged that we could use the yard to play in. So we'd play softball there, we were allowed to do that.

**AW:** But that was before the grave stones were leveled? Were they already put down?

**VK:** They were down, yeah. Kids would do whatever they wanted. They'd roam there, play as kids do. I remember one day there, I knew a couple of kids that were sort of my friends, in fact we later had a band together in those days, as kids, but they said, we hate this guy — this guy's a, I don't think they said he's a commie, but they might have said that this guy's commie and a bad guy. They were looking at this piece of paper, and they were crumpling it up, and I said, wait a minute, who is that and what is that you've got there? And they showed me this piece of paper that said "Ted Berrigan" on it.

**AW:** What?

**VK:** They didn't know who he was, there was no picture of him or anything. It was just kids' ignorance. But it was funny, I said, I know him, he's a great guy, what are you talking about? It was a flyer for a reading.

**AW:** I'm glad there were flyers with poets' names on them that were available. Well, they must have gotten it off the door. I do remember in high school this wonderful teacher, who was a great fan of Wallace Stevens's; he would read Stevens's poems aloud, and that was radical, as you can imagine. I think that was where I started to hear, particularly "The Idea of Order at Key West" — "She sang beyond the genius of the sea ... For she was the maker of the song she sang" — all those sounds and a certain real attraction to that.

**VK:** That's a simple but powerful teaching tool, hearing and reading something aloud. In my time, in a world you were intimately involved in, John Giorno's records, the Giorno Poetry Systems albums, were really important to me. Paul and Elio Schneeman and I used to listen to them, and there were certain tracks that we listened to over and over, like John Ashbery reading "The Tennis Court Oath." The sound of it is so much a part of it, and if you're not getting that in school, you're only getting half. Now of course, there's much more audio that's easily accessible, but then there wasn't.

**AW:** No there wasn't, and that was such an impetus for the Poetry Project. We needed a space for that aural and vocal projection. It speaks to how communities develop when you have social scenes with public performances. It gives young people a ground they can start from. And that word "project" as in "projective verse," talk about the double entendre, but to project poetry, the Poetry

Pro-ject. I'm going to start saying it like that again. Reading the Duncan-Levertov letters, at one point, I realized these folks were really listening to one another and a reel-to-reel or cassette tape might circulate. Paul Blackburn was recording the readings on his very heavy Wollensak, and some of those recordings still exist. A mention of a tape's being sent around, going to Creeley and Duncan and so on, that was important to this new American poetry. Not that anyone was thinking of it that way, but some kind of aspirational energy toward the "kinetics of the thing" (Olson) particularly in the alternative schools. Friendships, really communities that valued hearing a tape, just had a different valence. Ted would sometimes make off with the Poetry Project cassettes like our collaborative reading of

"Memorial Day" in 1976. I finally got a copy years later from Clark Coolidge, who had copied it as it circulated.

**VK:** So when the Project started in 1966, what were the other possibilities for hearing new poetry in New York?

**AW:** Well, the Café Le Metro readings and those open readings were moved into the church by 1965, spearheaded in a sense by Paul Blackburn and Ishmael Reed. There was a need because of political differences specifically at the Metro between the poets and the owners, thus a need to find alternative space. The 92nd St. Unterberg Poetry Center YMHA was happening, occasional things at N.Y.U., but nothing that you would normally go to as a much younger person. Some galleries. I remember a downtown gallery reading with Frank O'Hara and Jim Brodey. My first reading (with Lewis Warsh) was at Izzy Young's Folklore Center in the Village, I think in 1966 or '67. Very small space with just a few tiny hard wooden benches to sit on. It was exciting to be around other poets and artists.

**VK:** That's a whole other important part of readings – the social scene. How did you and other people that you were talking to see poetry in relation to the rock and roll that was happening at the time? I always saw a connection, and rock people from that era often reference poetry when they speak about those times.

**AW:** Of course, I absolutely think it was connected; I certainly felt connected. The poetry and music and music-with-poetry and other hybrids in performance were off the same tree, the same rhizome. The cultural interventions of Dylan, The Beatles, The Stones, were phenomenal, generative. We shared a world. And we were making a world too. Allen was an example for me — picking up musicians at every stop, possessed by his own sound, off key or no, putting Blake to music, paying serious attention to Dylan, who was a genius to him, because he could hear all the syllables. Seeing the inherent possibilities with music and poetry in performance. McClure knew Janis Joplin and Jim Morrison, wrote songs and poems for them. I traveled with Allen on Dylan's Rolling Thunder Revue in the mid-'70s. Allen was a key link to many of the great rock and roll artists, so many of them were reading him and Kerouac and William Burroughs and were "called" by their work.

**VK:** What about the Velvet Underground?

**AW:** Absolutely. Another radical intervention. The Velvet Underground were right down the block on St. Mark's Place at the Dom — the Electric Circus — thus very present, and Gerard Malanga, a close friend and poet, was in the show cracking his whip. Sometimes people would end up in the apartment after a show. Lou Reed was around the Project, and we published his work in *The World*. His mentor had been the soulful Delmore Schwartz. Lou was extremely well read — Yeats, T.S. Eliot, Burroughs. The Velvets' sound was strident, down under, mesmerizing, and came out of a dark left-hand path. And then later, the very lyrical Jim Carroll, whose favorite poet and influence was Frank O'Hara. Patti Smith was political, Romantic, redemptive, shamanic, invoking Rimbaud and Sinbad and the working class — "Piss Factory." Lou, Patti, Jim, Laurie Anderson did some of their first performances at The Poetry Project.

**VK:** That was great, Patti's anniversary reading, that you introduced, of the first time she read. That was the first time she performed in public, right? It was at the Project.

**AW:** Right, the 40th anniversary, that's amazing to me. How far we've traveled and yet how true to the original ethos and practice of "changing the frequency," as it were, and giving and having been given public space for that. Patti is a kind of mirror for me of our time. In rock and roll there was a move via music and collaborative energy toward a larger public. The poets have a continuum of obsession with prosody and more complicated text. Many of them were fiercely active, as you were saying, listening to these John Giorno recordings, or going to readings, and feeling that sense of the power of the text alone, text and voice. At least for us as readers and listeners with our particular attuned ears, there was something that was enough in the music of the language in and of itself, not needing additional support. People were trying to do these longer structures and certain kinds of invented genres that required different modes of dailiness and attention and different shapes on the page than a more rock-driven lyric could provide. Not that they don't overlap. What I've always enjoyed is having those long structures and then being able to break into a pattern that's more like a song, being musical throughout but having specific places where there's an intervention of a more direct or simple thing that can be quite arresting, depending on how it moves.

**VK:** The thing about rock and pop music in general is you really can't take the lyrics or the music apart from each other. There's a chemical reaction, when you get both together, that makes the combination greater than the individual parts. But how about this idea of seeing that we've been talking about? We've been doing a lot of visual seeing, but seeing of course is metaphorical too. How is poetry a vehicle for seeing?

**AW:** Poetry penetrates your being in a way that heightens sense perceptions. You see more, you can see beyond. You feel inner eye and ear change in relationship to language and to consciousness. I notice sometimes, reading poetry, and then going out, that other things, unlike poetry, are jarring, ragged, abrupt, because it's a different language on the street, the ordinary traffic of language, very simple, communicative: pass me the salt, I need a ticket. We inherit that relative quotidian demand, but you have to bring that into your magic spells and weave. Anselm Hollo's line "always treat language as a dangerous toy" comes to mind, or Alice Notley's "don't let the Tyrant fool you," and suddenly you are with a woman with a red sash and an owl on a shamanic voyage. Intense lucid dreaming and certain vectors of seeing operate, where you have myriad consciousness, the ear/eye attuned to very small moves, more intricate moves within individual words. A message that is fractured and interrupted, coming in and out of focus, engenders a different way of thinking and seeing: fractals, parts of objects, of beings, of landscape. Obviously, the attraction to reading and the necessity of semantic value persists, whether you deconstruct it or not. Words as signs and signals are always potent and complicated; maybe they are a "killer virus" as

Burroughs indicates. How it sets up images relates to visual art, and that is interesting. Walking around with you today, we're reading these paintings. We're reading objects, in this case up against human flesh and bodies, we're reading architecture, and we have an association with being human ourselves, when something's sleepy or languid or droopy, or plastic or precise. When something is cutting like Williams's flower, the edges of the flower cutting into space. The imagery that goes with poetry also has that ability to make these pictures in our minds. I don't know that visual artists are seeing it so differently — they're also caught up in the actual elements of making the work.

**VK:** Maybe each medium feels this about itself, but I sometimes feel a little bit of the lack of materials in poetry, compared to, say, this is an object on the wall. You can deny it, you can criticize it, but still it's a real physical, sensual thing. And then music has that sensual aspect that you feel in your body. And poetry has that when it's read aloud.

**AW:** Poetry feels most like life: fleeting, impermanent. You have to catch it in your mind. You can't own it. What I like in music is how abstract it is, you can't translate it easily to words. Sometimes they seem very harmonically caught up, or dissonantly disengaging and flying apart, the language and the music. Poetry travels light. What do you really need? A little tape recorder and a pencil. An Olivetti typewriter (I had Frank O'Hara's ex-typewriter for a while!). Art on walls and in spaces is grounding, more occupying, reassuring perhaps. And easier to talk about. Critics seem to have to go to French critical theory and philosophy to talk about poetry.

**VK:** One of the positive things I've found is that poetry, unlike the other arts, can exist perfectly intact on the web. If you read a poem on the web it's the same as reading it in a book or anywhere else, even to an extent hearing it on the web — the sonorities are not as important as they would be with a piece of music, where if it's using acoustics you want to hear it live. And artwork, unless it's something created for the web, you really can't see it on the web. Poetry in that mode comes out ahead!

**AW:** It does! I still like to have books of poetry or magazines because I can flip back. I don't like scrolling up and down, so there's a difference in the experience. The tactile experience with books is inestimable. Books are art objects in and of themselves. But I agree: the poem enters the head in any case and I do read a lot online.

**VK:** Do you have a Kindle or an iPad?

**AW:** Not yet. Do you recommend one?

**VK:** For books that are not poetry I hate the Kindle, because I read flipping back and forth. I flip to the index, I flip through non-fiction books, stuff like that I read jumping around. But ironically, I have found for poetry it really works. I got a Phillip Whalen book on the Kindle, and compared to these books of prose, the poems are 1 or 2 pages long, and that's fine, I get a complete experience easily.

**AW:** I have to try it. I can see how that would actually work.

**VK:** What about the painters, which painters were you hanging out with in the early days, and whose work were you seeing in galleries and museums?

**AW:** I had gone to Bennington, so there were many artists in and around that realm. David Smith I think died the year I arrived. Ken Noland was around. And on faculty: Jules Olitski, Anthony Caro. The immortal Joe Brainard became a close friend in 1967. The immortal George Schneeman also. Donna Dennis was living across the street on St. Marks Place. Alex Katz, Philip Guston, Larry Rivers, Jane Freilicher, Rudy Burckhardt, Yvonne Jacquette, Fairfield Porter were a part of the New York School nexus. I saw Willem and Elaine de Kooning, Vito Acconci, John Button, Richard Tuttle, Claes Oldenburg, Jim Dine, James Rosenquist. These were artists one had contact with on the premises of readings, gallery openings, loft parties. Andy Warhol, bigtime. One was seeing these artists and their work regularly. Some of these folks, like Joe and George, were close collaborators and were key to the *Angel Hair* magazine and books and *The World* publications. And we had covers from Alex and Yvonne and Philip Guston as well. Jim Dine did a magnificent cover for *BUN*, Rosenquist for Peter Schjeldahl's *Dreams*. So much generosity there. An amazing time. And one could visit studios, sit for portraits. Visual overload, so much variety, and so much paint.

I remember how Joe Brainard gave me and Lewis (Warsh) a terrific choice of drawings for Lee Harwood's *The Man with Blue Eyes*, and because we were using this elegant Fabriano paper for the *Angel Hair* magazine covers, I selected a subtle blue for the drawing we chose which was mainly lettering. I never checked with Joe, who, of course, as I later realized, was expecting the cover to be white! He was used to black and white mimeo. He was surprised but remarkably polite and amused about it all. I felt stupid and obvious about the "blue."

Tell me a Joe Brainard story.

**VK:** Joe I knew as a kid. He was always very generous, very warm, as were most of the poets I knew then. Joe once, for my birthday, gave me a shopping bag full of presents. Each was individually wrapped and labeled by Joe, in that inimitable handwriting of his, with a different date. So for the whole summer, I was opening one present a day from Joe. And they were amazing things — a flattened Coca Cola bottle, appliqué flowers, a cigarette lighter in the form of a miniature Campbell's soup can. Seen in retrospect, they relate directly to his art and his version of an appropriation of Pop culture. They had that, but they were also the recognition of what would make someone happy, what a kid would like. In that sense, they partake of Frank O'Hara's "Personism." How deeply would you say the New York poets of your generation were invested with O'Hara's ethos?

**AW:** We loved "Personism" and its breezy yet spot on ethos. It made what we do seem perfectly natural and entwined with our lives and humanness (how someone looks, their sexiness). Making someone happy. Like Joe always did. He lived the ethos. I remember Joe's gifts too — little cloth bag with miniature art works, the presentation — like your shopping bag — very exciting. I still wear the Victorian serpent rings with their ruby and diamond eyes — which came in elegant boxes — on my wedding finger. The New York School was permeated with generosity and sociability. And friendship. I was blessed at an early age. This as the *sacra conversazione* that take places in Italian Renaissance paintings. It was so important to wake up and talk and see and hear the poems of friends and wander to their studios and see the work and have the high talk and the high gossip and (sharped-tongued quips too) and the double entendres. I don't find that sharp wit everywhere. Frank O'Hara was so very attentive the two times I met him. And he raised the level of the frequency to a heightened awareness. He was interested, he was amused. He was on. And he noticed everything. Ted was the best at conveying Franks's "transmission" and had his own inimitable and grand and lovable style. He could make you better — how you thought and talked and rose to any occasion. Ted and other cohorts had seen much more of Frank in action. The elegance and sharpness of Tony Towle, Brodey's wild earthiness. Emanations of Frank? This was an amazing time and the poem was between persons and you went on your nerve. It was all art. I love that Allen and Amiri (LeRoi) are in this manifesto as well. That is a huge view — a confident view — that includes these giants. Talk about your own stirrings to poetry, your friendship with the Schneemans, your first magazine.

**VK:** George was different for me. He was both the father of my friends — Paul, Elio, and Emilio (now Emil) — and an artist living among and collaborating, on an almost daily basis, with poets. I was very familiar with his work as an artist and designer of poetry book and magazine covers. He created an intimate, quietly subversive zone of visual complement to what the poets were doing. His images, which often included quotations in the form of collaged elements from 1930s magazines, showed him to be one of the most sensitive early readers of the poetry of Ted, Ron, you, Bill, Larry, Alice, and many others.

I was always turned on by poetry, even as a child. I loved poetry classes in school; it didn't even matter what the poetry was. In sixth grade, we had to memorize one poem a week, a useful discipline. I make use of memorization until today, and there was a period, in my thirties, when I would memorize entire readings in order to focus on the performance as though it were a musical performance. In the seventh or eighth grade, we had a poetry class which again I really responded to. I recently found the textbook we used. It was called *Some Haystacks Don't Even Have Any Needle*, and it attempted to introduce the students to contemporary poetry; it had Roethke and Updike but also Antin, Blackburn, Levertov, and Snyder. And it had artwork by de Kooning, Kienholz and others that related to the poetry, which was printed in a sans serif font. It was trying to be real, not cute, and I respected that. I particularly liked the Blackburn poem, "The Stone," as it traversed an area of downtown, from 9th and Stuyvesant to West Broadway, that was known to me and felt specific: "…there were pigeons / circling / over the buildings at / West Broadway, and over them a gull…" By ninth grade, I had started going to the Poetry Project, so all bets were off. I had met Paul Schneeman, who joined my school in the ninth grade, and along with two other students, Kate Hammon and Liam Fennelly, and Elio Schneeman, who went to another school, we formed a poetry cohort of our own. It was totally spontaneous and full of the thrill of discovery. Poetry as pure pleasure! It was then we would spend hours listening to the Giorno Poetry Systems LPs, reveling in the sonorities of all the poets' voices. But this activity was totally natural to us. It, along with writing poetry, going to readings, discussing poetry, and sharing our poems, editing them together, was seamlessly incorporated into listening to rock and roll, eating, hanging out, going to the movies, and all the other things teenagers like to do.

I always wrote, from about the age of seven on. I wrote a lot of stories early on, but more and more, as I read publications like *Adventures in Poetry* and *The World*, I began to see how writing could take on an experimental aspect that served its own needs, so to speak, without any ulterior motive, such as telling a story. Larry Fagin even published something I wrote, rules to a football board game I created, in *Adventures in Poetry* when I was 10. There was a lot of support from the poets' community. Kenward Elmslie once put a sheet of onionskin in his typewriter and said he was going to type on it anything I said. "What do you want me to say?" I asked. He typed "What do you want me to say?" I realized the game was on, there was no escaping, so I became more conscious and conscientious about what was coming out of my mouth. I was aware, too, that the clock was ticking. This wasn't going to last forever. It was a game we were playing that would end at a certain point. When we reached the end of the page, Kenward pulled the sheet out of the typewriter and gave it to me. A priceless lesson in generosity and the freedom that should accompany the writing process, that can be spurred by a sense of its communal possibilities.

Our first magazine, *Open Window*, was edited by Paul and me, and we published our friends but also reached out to Jim Carroll, Jimmy Schuyler, Ted, John Yau, Bob Rosenthal, Simon Schucat, and Steven Hall, who all gave us work to publish. It was learning by example. We saw the mimeo mags and heard about how they were made. We got artists, friends and colleagues, to do the covers. We saw that magazine-making was community-building, though we wouldn't have expressed it in those terms! That was 1976-78. After that, I took a long break from publishing. Later, inspired by many others active in the world of poetry publishing as survival, I decided to start up again, and that became *Vanitas*.

Anne, talk a little about your sense of community — the difference between the early days, when you found your company of like-minded individuals, and how it is now, with so much friendship going on digitally, extended beyond the screens we all use to communicate.

**AW:** That wonderful sense of game, "the occasion of these ruses," as Frank O'Hara says in a more serious vein. Yes, the community has expanded, and there are a few more generations. And I have 40 years of The Kerouac School at Naropa, the quirky gifted active people that have passed through that ring of poetic fire. Staying in touch as a guardian ring of communal art and sanity seems more important now than ever, as the world gets weirder, more troubled, violent, endangered. We need to encircle, protect the realms of imagination and art with the heart and mind, as Frank did, as Joe did. The technology can aid us, but the spirit has to be there. The commitment to standing in virtual space, if need be, as a force-field, an alternative vision of how to be alive — that's still person-to-person.

**VK:** Speaking of person-to-person, what about some of your collaborations with artists?

**AW:** The work with Richard Tuttle was interesting. He'd heard me read "Makeup on Empty Space" and envisioned a 3D box with a magic lantern that came out of his meditation on this phrase. It evolved in a collaborative weekend with a Chinese opera director, a makeup artist, a musician, and my role directing and augmenting the text in a performance in rural upstate NY. The Kaldewey Press made a beautiful box that manifests the performance, includes videotape, audio tape, plus images of the actor with makeup designed by Tuttle.

I liked being the text person. On call in a spirit of serendipity and improv, and yet it becomes a very located, magical object. It was a different time. One was used to walking into Joe Brainard's loft, George Schneeman's apartment, unannounced and spontaneously making a work of art. George would pull out a sheet of Arches paper, bits from old magazines and music scores that he saved. I would pull out a couple of lines I had, or I'd write something, and we'd improvise from there, with erasure, addition, on the spot. And that would lead to a delicious home-cooked Italian meal!

I'd walk around with Ted, and we'd drop in on Larry Rivers. He did a collage of us for a reading. Companionability. Rosenquist, Alex, or Jane Freilicher would provide artwork for flyers or book covers. The exchange was not mediated by a gallery. It was facilitated by living in the same neighborhood and our friendship.

With Pat Steir, we worked at the Brodsky Center at Rutgers with their master printer, Randy Hemminghaus. It is a folded scroll entitled *Cry Stall Gaze*. I wrote the text for Pat. She was talking about Sol LeWitt, who had been her partner and had recently died. The pouring of emotion, pouring of the pain. That image turned into an 18-page poem. I feel an alliance, an affinity, with Pat's influences. She speaks of Cage often. Something in her spiritual ethos. She studied ink drawing in Japan and China. She creates monumental works in spaces that are like altered dimensions. Working in a book format is a challenge. But even in that smaller format there is something awe-inspiring, Promethean. The way she works, climbing on her ladder, is very physical.

**VK:** Would you characterize her paint application as controlled or Dionysian?

**AW:** Somewhere in between. We are those who "love to be astonished," as Lyn Hejinian puts it. That is my connection with Pat — we love to be astonished.

Kiki Smith has a sculpture called *The Girl*, which echoes the themes of my new book, *Voice's Daughter A Heart Yet to be Born*. Kiki sent me a photo of a fragment of the sculpture, saying it represented the future, a kind of future-body. That led to our using images of the sculpture and motifs from it in the book. I have consistently pushed collaboration, with text or image or music. It's one of the joys of my life.

**VK:** Let's detail some of the other shows we saw on our walks together, keeping in mind there are many more to come.

**AW:** Emile Clark's works have a dizzying vibrancy. Her particulars, her extraordinary hand for the drawing, the line, the bursting forth as it were of new life forms. She always brings up that sense of co-existing interconnectedness of palpable living things, organisms. I see into my own raw (untapped) emotions in her work, which might sound odd. What I might be capable of if I lived out in the rugged untamed landscape without no humans.

I feel more animal next to a Richard Serra.

I would like to enter Donna Dennis's little houses as I dream. I think I've been there.

I liked some of the documentation pieces — John Cage & Laurie Anderson — at Holly Solomon's entrepreneurial stable show. I think that kind of work is needed in the archive of the timeframes, always.

**VK:** As we slip out the door, any thoughts on seeing per se and what visual artists bring to our sense of how live now?

**AW:** With seeing, there's that first hit, primordial, scary . . . eye hits object and object hits back! Something is refreshed and triggered when it's working, that first hit.

Satori! Plug in the socket. Then reasoning kicks in and chain of reference and projection and history and vocabulary and precedent and attitude. And you want to walk around and feel all the dimensions. 1 or 2 or 3 let it sink in, see the different angles, lighting, and your mood for it too. Paintings and caryatids. Hovering entities, elemental. Star dust. Time might stop. Sensual, intellectual, pleasing, and close. Edwin Denby brought things closer to me. Dancers' moves so demanding from Balanchine. Imbricated realities. Out on the street now. Looking up to building and sky. Feel the preciousness of this mechanism we have for form, for the flux of our metabolism in and around it, our curiosity for it and making of it, as in *poiesis*, and the matrix of our inclination — towards what? Solidification, gnosis, haunting of the material world and its stubborn impermanence? A kind of drama perhaps making us more alive: taking a walk to look at art with you.

**Notes**

Frontispiece: *Beauty,* a 1911 sculpture by Frederick MacMonnies. She rests on the winged horse Pegasus, symbolizing poetic inspiration, under an inscription taken from "The Shadow and the Light," by John Greenleaf Whittier.

Page 26: Deborah Kass with pulp, ink., *I Wanna Rock With You,* part of "After Hours: Murals on the Bowery," presented by Art Production Fund and the New Museum, 2011.

Page 32: Photomontage, including photograph of Anne Waldman reading in Oh! Sandy: A Remembrance, at "Come Together: Surviving Sandy, Year 1," Industry City, Brooklyn, November 10, 2013.

Page 39: Anne Waldman with Donna Dennis' 1976 sculpture *Tourist Cabin Porch,* at "Hooray for Hollywood!" exhibition, at Mixed Greens and Pavel Zoubok galleries, 2014.

Page 44: Anne Waldman at Alex Katz' exhibition at Gavin Brown's enterprise, 2014.

Page 46 (left image): Kerstin Brätsch artwork at Gavin Brown's enterprise, 2014.

Page 47: Anne Waldman at Larry Poons exhibition at Danese/Corey gallery, 2014.

Page 48: Richard Serra installation at Gagosian Gallery, 2014.

Made in the USA
Middletown, DE
10 November 2016